Locust and Marlin considers how, in candle's burn, we tell our stories and live and love. Where is the origin, our point in space from which we view the world? How much control do we have over who we are and what impact we have on the territory we inhabit? In a world whose boundaries and pathways are increasingly difficult to define, how do we find our way home?

JL Williams was born in New Jersey, studied at Wellesley College and received a distinction on the M.Litt in Creative Writing at the University of Glasgow. She has been published in journals including *Edinburgh Review, Fulcrum, Magma, Poetry Wales, Stand* and *The Wolf.* Her poetry has been translated into Greek, French and Dutch and she has translated poetry from Spanish and Greek.

Her poems have been featured in the *New Writing Scotland 30* anthology and in the Scottish Poetry Library's *Best Scottish Poems 2011* anthology. She was awarded a grant from the Scottish Arts Council for a poetry collaboration entitled *chiaroscuro pentimenti* with composer Martin Parker and artist Anna Chapman, and the Edwin Morgan Travel Bursary from the Scottish Arts Trust.

In September 2009 she journeyed to the Aeolian Isles to write a collection inspired by Ovid's *Metamorphoses* called *Condition of Fire.*

JL Williams plays in the band Opul and is Programme Manager at the Scottish Poetry Library. Her website is at www.jlwilliamspoetry.co.uk

Also by JL Williams

Condition of Fire

JL Williams

Locust and Marlin

Shearsman Books

First published in the United Kingdom in 2014 by
Shearsman Books
50 Westons Hill Drive
Emersons Green
BRISTOL
BS16 7DF

Shearsman Books Ltd Registered Office
30–31 St. James Place, Mangotsfield, Bristol BS16 9JB
(this address not for correspondence)

www.shearsman.com

ISBN 978-1-84861-328-7

Acknowledgements
Special thanks to my family, especially Marilyn Gaesser,
Peter and Pat Brailey and the Iremongers.

Cover image by Anupa Gardner,
reproduced by permission of the artist
Copyright © 2014, Anupa Gardner.
www.anupagardner.com

Contents

Heron	11
November's Song	12
A Tender Still	13
Like Phaeton	14
Learning to Love the Present	17
Spirals	18
Flutter	19
Resurrection	20
Forum Magnum	21
All Water	22
Water Phoenix	24
Nor Loch	25
Body of Stone	26
Storm	27
Tonight	28
Locust and Marlin	29
Last Night When I Died	30
Last Night When I Fell in Love	32
Sargasso Sea	33
Sand	35
Creation	36
Locust King	37
Waltzer	38
Hotel	39
Hateful Shell	40
"…where wings have memory of wings"	41
Two Legs, Two Arms	45
Stone Song	46
Instead of Rushing	47
Blinding	48
Relativity	49
Stones of the West	50
Barn Door	51
Homecoming	52

The Dark Spiral and the Spiralling Light   53
Because You Are   54
Triptych   55
Legacy   58
Horizon   59
Home   60
Cathedral   61
The Veil   62
Metonymy   63
Corpus   66
La Faccia   67
You Learn How Beautiful You Are   68
As if You Were Homeland   69
A Little Light   70
Isn't the Start   72
Person   73
Sightings   74
Son   75
Revelation   79

for James Iremonger

in whose heart I've found my home

&

for Stewart Laing

poet of space

And the shapes of the locusts were like unto horses prepared unto battle;
and on their heads were as it were crowns like gold,
and their faces were as the faces of men.
　　　—Revelation 9:7, *King James Bible*

The surest sign of wonder is exaggeration. And since the inhabitant of a
shell can amaze us, the imagination will soon make amazing creatures,
more amazing than reality, issue from the shell.
　　　—Gaston Bachelard, *The Poetics of Space*

Heron

Imagine a great silence
whose wings touch no branches.

Imagine a space demarcated
by lack of sound.

It flies very low to the water.
It stands very still when it lands.

Its strange beak opens.

November's Song

They took her down to the river,
held her mouth for pouring in.

The light through leaves.
A day like this.

Success can't be defined by whether
milk comes out of the milkweed's
squeezed bud. Or downy messages.
Honey from the honeysuckle's slid prick
sometimes touches the tongue.

A kind of music invented that day
of scattered leaves,
the bashed song of her hair.

A Tender Still

It was down by the river.
It was down where the fish get gutted
after being slammed on the boat-side.

A drowned mouse made
the world seem very big.

I kneeled, nearly, to see him.

The dirt was mucked
with leaf matter, half-dug roots.

I wanted to blow
life back into it but
the body was an old thing.

The river flowed.

Like Phaeton

1

There you are crying like a dog.
How does a dog cry?
Sliding on its ass to the sea,
sliding on a slide of tears and dog water,
sliding down sawgrass slicked to
sliced edges glassed with dog salt, diamond-hard
edges like fingernails that could cut glass.

There you are crying, throwing your tears
to one side and the other,
throwing tears to break them against a brick wall
so in slow-motion tears explode into globes,
each globe a glass ball flying through air
reflecting your gesture of frustration your arms
cast out at your sides *your face contorted.*

There you are crying like a dog,
feeling you're sliding down a bank toward the sea, afraid,
frustrated by the fact of your crying cuz a man
shouldn't cry, a woman or a dog
are the right sort of creatures for crying, for weakness, for
emoting when beaten but
wasn't it a woman said that to you in the first place?

Suddenly, mid-tumult, you remember
your father crying in a room of books,
books packing walls on shelves of oak,
his body a recognisable shape
outlined by shafts of sun
flickering with each shudder of pain-torn core.

2

My dad started talking about a chopper.
I licked my lip, first-furred, savouring
the salt-tang, lemon, margarita.

Wanted a cigarette, knew he wouldn't
approve. The bartender joked
with a local at the end of the long bar.

It was that kind of summer
when sunset mixes with the fake light
in the room, makes everything *glowing*.

He stopped then, said he couldn't… go on.
It jarred, the image of him
hanging, laying his eyes on, something.

3

He.

He. He.

He does not have the eyes from your dream.

He does not have the skin you imagine.

He does not speak
as others do.

He does not stand long in the light
but walks away toward the source of it becoming
less of a figure and more of a point
around which light flickers.

Learning to Love the Present

And I can't *not* think of the remorse of Oedipus,
    —Frank Bidart, *California Plush*

This time, when you fall down, get up again.

I mean he's going to knock you down that's
his job that's what he gets paid to do we all
have to make a living *isn't that weird.* There must have been
some time when you could have found food in the forest but now
it's the flashing bulbs and the *gnarl gnarl* of the men in the hats and
that's your blood rolling past your eye on the mat but
can you hear that music?

It sounds like
yeah
Coney Island, the girl with the pink balloon, no
I know we're not there anymore but here she is smelling of
rubber and cotton candy and cotton panties washed in
water scented with lilacs,
also that seaweedy smell from sitting on sand.
Look how her eyes go all wide and owl-like when the freaks
    parade by,
the bearded lady and the two boys attached at the waist and there…
just round the corner of the hot dog stand by the Ferris wheel,
your father playing the mandolin
and a monkey with bells round his tiny ankles, dancing.

Get up. Get up for the next blow, friend.

Spirals

Life in each stone,
as bright as ours,
that much is known.

Like a bone
some marrow powers
life in each stone.

For that atoned
there will be flowers.
That much is known.

The sparrow flown
past all our hours.
Life in each stone.

With each rock thrown
we threaten towers.
That much is known.

Try lying prone while rainfall showers.
Life in each stone,
that much is known.

Flutter

They broke open her ribcage
to let out the birds.

The birds were mostly black…
some brown, some grey.

The birds flew up like a cough.
They fell like stones.

Across the valley, a boy broke open a stone.
He examined the crystal interior skin and wept.

She came up behind him.
She laid her hand on his chest.

By reaching around him he felt
her blood purple hardness.

The heart in him cried,
"Cuh-caw, cuh-caw, cuh-caw."

Resurrection

If I were a snail inside its shell
and winter came with all its howl
then hell I'd bury myself in mud

and build a wall to keep the chill
where it belongs in water's heart
and sleep for all the months of dark

until the black slime told it's time
and then I'd crack the seal and rise
as if reborn to bathe in sun.

Were it so easy for a man.

Forum Magnum

In the space made by the white walls of the Forum
civilised people walk in leather sandals
as people will walk for many years to come.

Years, days. In memory it is your hand
dangling the silver chain
that glints in the sun. Birds.

Discussion at the feet of a great thinker.
The smell of rain on wind down from Palatine.
You always came with rain. Birds,

a change in the weather much like the sort of relief
sleep brings from waking, waking,
sleep. Via Sacra, footsteps.

All Water

Been thinking a lot about gills,
how this flesh fringe can take in

water and air, how you can
catch a fish by tickling it

under its belly wearing silk
stockings on your hands.

How you can hold a fish
gently in the current's stream,

revive it
as if it were a lover

needing stroking, needing
the brush of lips over glazed skin.

What is it we do
when we take a fish or sip,

pluck an apple, kill a man
or beast? Are we stopping or continuing

an endless flow
whose movement is toward

home or origin, whatever that may be,
whatever that may be, home,

beginning, but what or where is this?
Was it a cloud that formed,

let the first pure diamond
drop from its wet womb? Was it

first the puddle evaporating
in billion years' young sun?

Is this why
everything keeps moving, why

the circle within the circle
within the circle turns?

Because there is no soil
worth dying for (it'll

have us soon enough). We
are mostly water and all water

is a thing that seeks a home but has no home
except that carved in earth by seeking.

Water Phoenix

A wealth of documentation could be assembled on the
subject of "resurrection shells".
—Gaston Bachelard, *The Poetics of Space*

I've ground the bodies of the dead
and dropped them in the wavelets, watched
them live again.

The life force in the grain remains
no matter what you do to them.
You say it is their brothers come.

But look how they materialise
as if from nothing but what was
alive… it must be, it must be them spinning.

Nor Loch

Lilac past its best, wet air
sticky with a sick perfume.

Wind in sodden trees, green
grass that white moths drown in.

The fountain flooded.
The rubbed-out castle
aching above the graveyard, its bones soaking
in the eidolon of water.

Body of Stone

When I was a stone, my heart was stone.
My foot was a foot-shaped stone.

You sat with my stone hand in your lap
wondering who made such things
as a stone liver, a stone stomach, a stone eye.

When I was a stone
I felt the story of other stones
in my mouth;

striated, striated—
but it sounded like gravel underfoot
or a storm of pebbles.

The movement of the winds and the tide
affected me as emotions do
small children but I never cried.

You realised I was able to change
and that was how I came to be
something other than stone.

But sometimes when I wake in the night,
your back to my back,
I am stone.

Storm

Sand in the eyes,
the mouth.

Wind so high
it lifts the beach.

The clenched fist
cleaved by shell.

Waves break and coil,
cough froth.

A bird flies backwards.
Worry, sand-like, swirls.

Tonight

In the forest of old firs,
no one will walk but owls
opening and closing their wings
on needle-strewn paths.

No candles will light in the church manse.
Miners will lay down their picks.
The earth will turn on its axis
while people are sleeping.

In outer space cells of the sun
will collapse in explosions of gold gas
while dark clear holes open
where the heat is intense.

Somewhere a boat on an ocean
will rock back and forth on a slow wave
making a sound like the gentle
breath of a child.

South winds will rise
and the scent of black orchid
will wend its way toward heather
sequestered in ice.

Locust and Marlin

In my father's old bait and tackle shop
giant fish dangle from hooks near the men
grinning from ear to ear in the grainy,
soiled photographs clipped from newspapers

years ago before these same brave fishers
were diagnosed one by one with disease
or crippling forgetfulness or pains
brought on by the drag of time's bright lure.

Inaudible prophets—dust minnows swim
in slides of dull light that call up dad's ghost;
"Locust will fall in a plague of legions,
summon avengers from all the world's seas,

phalanx of marlin clear the wave's belly,
angels with no tongue and spears for faces."

Last Night When I Died

I died in my sleep last night
or was sent to my death.

It was too cold
and my friend was walking me to the train.

I wanted
more than anything a cigarette.

She pulled out a pouch of tobacco.
Women in the dim alleyway

called like whores or wash maids
but it was strange

because it was so cold.
I fumbled with the fat cigarette,

she gave me a match.
It flared along the crag of the stone wall.

We came out from the narrow
close into a cobbled

square. I couldn't see
beyond the terminal but knew

there were trains waiting.
There was an old flip board with the number

11C on it, I think. That was my train.
I was grateful for the cigarette,

her company. She joked
as if trying to distract me but I could hear

strain in her voice. I spoke
of looking for one another,

of how we might
end up in the same place, that we

must try to remember each other's faces.
But to myself that sounded

implausible somehow,
as if I knew my face would not be the same.

Last Night When I Fell in Love

Like a thief or an old-time lover I snuck
into your family's house having walked

up a steep road through the city,
street lamps incandescing.

We feared your family would find me
but when they did it didn't matter.

Two younger brothers (you have none)
seemed friendly and shy but everyone

was disturbed; someone had just died.
We travelled fulgent morning

to shore and boarded a steamer,
sailing a firth past whales into sunrise.

On deck, a Romanesque balcony,
you wept,

apologised saying
a man shouldn't cry, your father

facing the water, his back to you,
my face and hands wet with your tears.

No, I said. No, cry.

Sargasso Sea

Whose angels are women confined to river water,
their hair green wool
spooling in gin-clear streams.

At dawn I watch
the wood envelop your body.

Hair in the river the heron steps on
with most delicate
precision.

Do the women weep?

Do tears salt
parr unseen from the bridge?

A sea whose only borders are currents;
eels born there swim for miles, migrate
overland to rivers where women
lie face down in the weir.

The fishes' curiosity; their fearless, cloying
love of all things standing.

You lower the cage of dead rabbits.
When you return ropes are wound round
the rubbery bodies of black eels.

The heron's stillness, his samurai coif,
his necklace of grey feathers.

Women in the water sing beneath his feet,
tell him where to stand,
where the fishes sleep.

At night our bodies
twine like cords of flesh.

Sand

Is it the sea that moans,
or wind in branches?

Walking the wood over dunes,
wind bends the pines.

Shells in sand
are filled with sand,
will be sand.

What will be in a hundred,
a thousand, a million years?

Sand, and likely wind
mouthing sky.

Creation

One dreamer thought a shell was made
by a creature turning somersaults, each turn
a room for the home.

The staircase spiralling upward
by the force of a leg.

I push against this wall.
An oyster spits and makes a shine.
I turn. What do I make?

The clam unfrets his valves,
claims its flesh food;
a mouth-like home.

I hold a shell to my ear.
It sings.

Locust King

From the height at which I drift in starless night
I look out on the cities of men undone,
my face a man's, my body almost horse,
my crown as like a cage as like a crown.

How many times I've been a home for names,
the past a constant pain not easily forgot.
Like this red moon my heart beams on an empty world
whose dreams are long since dead.

A music comes from where I do not know.
When I exhale the dust obscures my view.
Immortal as I am it is a curse
to be without you for all time.

And so again I make your perfect form,
and so again you die to be reborn.

Waltzer

See, from the hot air balloon,
floating like a wish in the blue sky,
how the battlefield is an ocean;
the meat of evolution
churned into a vast, ululating pool.

What rises is the skeleton of a man.

It is your bones, your doppelgänger—
your true self.

See how it waltzes in blood,
bites through the air as if air was fine-milled bread,
waves—you did not think it could see you but it can,
and as your eyes meet its holes,
you exchange places.

You stare up at the balloon.
You feel the red wind pass through you.
You breathe out steam.

Something falls from the sky.
What is it? You can almost make it out,
you can almost remember… that face.

Hotel

We enter a room with cabinets,
a chest of drawers.

My first instinct
to violate
each secret space.

What is the snail's nightmare?

I poke. I prod.
I pull the latch
like a hungry bird.

Hateful Shell

Snail of the sea,
mouth like a bag,
sucks up the slumbering
parrotfish.

Stabs it alive.
Digests it for tea.

Slithers off burping
blue tails and
blue fins and
rolling eyes.

"…where wings have memory of wings."

W.B. Yeats, *Upon a House Shaken by the Land Agitation*

1

Still, and quiet.
It takes 'a thing' to make a sound.
Is that true?
Is it true that every birdcall
comes from the mouth of a bird?

You die,
all the stars in the sky turn into eyes,
weep.

The flowers in the graveyard
dig their roots deeper.

There is a hill,
so there must be a valley.

There is a river
so there must be banks,
and a slow
erosion of earth;
pebble by pebble,
particle by particle,
past the fins of fishes
toward the sea.

2

You draw down the blackened branch,
what is left of your life—
you explain that this is truth and with its char
you trace that splendid word
onto the page, and cry,
and watch its lines tremble and swell.

3

To spit in the face of time
(that wetted clock),
to make a new myth and not explain
each detail of the womb from which it's born,
to bend the old harp to a new song—
to hammer hot metal until it bleeds
crimson stars on the black
shawl of earth,
to invite god to walk upon this earth
and burn his feet from white to black,
from black to white—
and admire the change in him.

4

The heart breathes.
The heart is transformed by drinking powder.
You stand up for the first time since you were a child.
You make a song like a flock of birds.
The heart breathes.

The hand turns red.
The red hand reaches the shore before the birds.
You stand up for the first time since you were born.
The heart breathes.
The mind winces.
No one can make you feel strange.
The battle rages beneath the eyes.
The heart is transformed by flowing water.
You smile.
The heart breathes.
The red hand makes an impression on the sand.
The bird spreads out its wings like a blessing to die.
You smile.
The heart breathes.
You stand up for the first time since you were dead.
You smile.
The heart is transformed by the realisation that you are alive.
The heart breathes.
You smile.
The heart breathes.
The heart breathes.
The heart breathes.

5

In the sea
there are fish that can fly
and birds that can swim.

Hold up the hand
and feel its bones
much like those of a bird.

The history of a people
is in its bones.

The bones remember
what it is to fly.

When they crack open
the sound they make
is the call of a bird.

Two Legs, Two Arms

It wasn't only as if
and when

and then and then

a white flower
a thousand then

a thousands flowers

and in their midst

an arm, a leg

a leg, an arm

a dream, a dream

Stone Song

My strange stone.
My dying stone.
My clinging stone.
My sugared stone.
My embarrassed stone.
My rosy stone.
My reflecting stone.
My burning stone.
My baying stone.
My exchanging stone.
My jasmine stone.
My killing stone.
My glowing stone.
My cobalt stone.
My bleeding stone.
My peaty stone.
My changing stone.
My keening stone.
My copper stone.
My believing stone.
My ribald stone.
My blue-bruised stone.
My coming stone.
My oiled stone.
My tender stone.
My almond stone.
My aching stone.
My whispering stone.
My ruby stone.
My holy stone.
My breathing stone.
My stone.
My stone.

Instead of Rushing

Water opted for stillness.
This was not in its nature, banks
(the lips of earth) crumbled.
Petals in pools; stars.

All over the world boats sat like fat cats
in sunshine. Sailors wept and cursed, the women
once wracked by tides took deep breaths, bled less,
kissed their men. Some comfort then in

pause. A bird creaks. Snow slides
from a mountaintop and melts a gush.
All flow starts then, pools to rivers' bends become
a never-ending oxbow round the world…

but something remains of peace, stillness;
puddles like mirrors.

Blinding

river turns the wheel

a hundred days of sunlight
glint off ivy

wheel grinds the grain

all this time spent
trying to be nothing

men sift the flour

light clings to froth
on the river's tongue

women knead the bread

water unveils
its secret

hungry mouths are fed

one to shine
one to see the shining

Relativity

The sea, grass, a garden.

Stones' mouths
open to rain.

Waves breathing salt
on old stone.

One stone says,
"How short life can be,"
but it seems
ironic considering
the nature of stone.

Stones of the West

But don't you gold?
Do you quartz, crystal?

We gave up everything
but breathing.

Jaded.

Barn Door

In that a goat might die and be reborn
as goat or as some other name or place
or sort of feeling, the look on a face,
the bend of an arm or fling
of a pillow or dress
across a low bed chosen carefully
for weight-bearing ability and response to stress;

in that this might be a local event
and attended by all, the lovers and the rich folk
and even the small man with the fork;
and even the poor, in that the goat might die
and be reborn for the poor with their glory
unsullied by having and honed by needing,
made ready for the opening of the door.

Homecoming

Like the entrance of a cave's mouth,
the dark hall warns me off.

I stand at the front door peering
into wilderness.

Some endless hole, the silence
of a thousand empty rooms.

My heart a wolf
howling into this void.

The Dark Spiral and the Spiralling Light

Both your names I know
but will not tell.

Both of you found in dunes
and nothing but shells—
nothing but shells I say but do not mean
nothing.

You once were palaces,
walls of royal spit and sweat excreted.

Exemplary toil. I dream of your
perfectly proportioned,
masterfully curving
rooms upon rooms—
dark dreams and dreams of light.

Because You Are

You do not have to feel alone.
The trees will open their barks for you
and invite you into their heart.

There you become the substance of wood
ageing in circles and never suffering fear
of season's end, for trees
diurnal revolution—passing—
is triumphant and commensurate with change.

Enter the trees with your centre first
and your bones will follow
in harmony with the way of all things.

Triptych

River Poem I / Sainthood

Her face was marked.

You laugh (wipe off the tear).
Destined? I wonder.
But no, we must say *accident*.

There was an accident that killed her need.
Well, her sight went. Or, her face
stained in the flood and she was sainted.

The Clydesdales in a high row,
their creamy fetlocks tossed with each step, steaming.
Clack, clack, like the gun shots. Clack, clack.

Yes, she was showing all the dirty boys
to tango. Drunken. They pulled her clothes off.
Gorgeous. It was her mission.

Don't worry. It was meant to be, (wave of the hand)
this story. Fatidic nightmares—the rising of rivers.

They went to protest and the police came.
It was a riot. The horses trod them.
They had been dancing.
On stones and skulls, the hooves knocked.
The rivers rose, the horses drowned.
Drowned the police. Drowned the bad boys.

We're painting triptychs to tell this story.
She cannot see but she remembers.

"Aye, quite scared of those horses.
It's for the best. And now the rivers
are not in danger. They showed their power."

She teaches tango by the river.
We watch her dancing from the patio
drinking gin laced with fresh water.

River Poem II / Internment

> "…Go, when you have had your supper;
> but come again in the morning, and bring us beautiful victims."
> —Telemachos, *The Odyssey of Homer*
> translated by Richard Lattimore

In the forest of memory she ground a path.
The white strands of her hair, her smile
familiar here; "Searching for the Nor Cat,"
she says or *I search for it…*

Here the pine brooms feather forehead, chest.
The amber tea of rivers steeped with pine roots weaves
a mazy tapestry to colour bodies, make them
smell of cardamom in wooden casks.

Grey spiders race the branches,
secret message carriers expressing out of silk the orders
whispered by the kings of forgotten stables,
often deadly words the like of

"Love what you kill" and
"Eat of that which is your inspiration."
This fretted wisdom cloaking in beauty
the dozy wanderer, the victim

ripe for elucidation.

River Poem III / Life

Lacuna where water was—
the place for being born.
I should explain.

Evolution is a parasite of death.
I've learned how water
leaves the earth, and then, comes back again.

He made love to me, here, in this hole.

You thought it wouldn't work this way.
I said, here, you put it here.

That's what we were taught
when your head was turned down
looking how you grew.

It's like a seed. You plant it
in this hole in the dirt and the water
comes up from the river to fill it.

No. Not love. Water, from the river.

Legacy

Prophet who escapes with few followers,
whose sons are Hope and Pillage—
these two flags of race,
without whom no ship can set sail.

Bound to the isle of winds
I will hatch them of moaning shells,
two wet wells;
the bleached volcanoes of age.

Come father, anoint my boys' lips
with fire; their burned tongues
will be our long ago future.

Horizon

What we see of the circle; an arc.

Below is there another half vibrating?

These planets whose golden mean
is sound.

Close your eyes and listen
not with your ears.

Listen.

Listen with your blossom of a heart.

Home

The colder the wind outside,
the cosier your fireside.

Comforting, the notion
of the rabbit in its burrowed hole.

The snail inside its shell,
the turtle,
the weaver in its hanging nest
able to rest.

Cathedral

Each tower owns a set of stairs
that spirals toward the sky.

Dizzying, the narrow, curling
climb to god

or birds whose home
is angel's breath.

Unfinished, I can only reach
the underbelly of a cloud.

Standing on the top step,
overlooking scaffolding

and heads absorbed in prayer, my own spins
at the thought of endlessness.

The Veil

I left the world to find the world that we had lost
and lost the world again, as one must, perhaps.
I never knew how beautiful my own country was.

We have a small space of time in which to touch.
There is a veil and beyond that
an old metal ornate grating
and the heat comes from there and the dreams.

The gears spin and no matter how often
these planets align it is you who must accommodate
to love the sensation of sunrise
because it will not rise forever, even in California
with the oranges dripping off the trees.

The ink runs out, or runs dry.
I learned to live, and now I am learning to die.
The taste of the juice on your lips…
that, I will never forget.

Metonymy

1

She comes again and again – you recognise her
as the lick of flame between dunes,
the one with shoulders
appearing like necks of swans.
The one who bends and is seen
again as willow or some fall of water,
needs more than the colour of winds to define
the effect she has on the atmosphere as she moves.

How to explain?

It is the man and his rib,
the woman and her egg, the man and his egg, the egg
and his eyes, the apple and the dinosaur and the bird and the frog
with no arms and legs, call it a snake,
call it the blame of ages.

She turns.

Like Flaubert, you see the ripe
mounds of her breasts.
Like Nabokov, you shape your lips to her name.
Like God, you refuse to speak.

She turns.

You see yourself in her eyes
whose colour changes, is a butterfly wing in a cabinet
coming miraculously back to life,

is not still pinned down, is making you think
of freedom, is turning more green as your shadow absorbs
    the light.

The alley behind the warehouse
whose end fades into moss
and white snowdrops…

she knows it,

how you sit there sometimes, downhearted,
dreaming of fire.

2

She is writing a story in which
she celebrates you
as the lover who never left,
who never got bored or expected more than her beauty,
who saw outside yourself to the woman beside you,
who found as you aged that your heart
fit even better her hand,
who touched her again in her blindness
and made her feel safe,
who read to her in the final night of her wandering

grace,

dunes of fluorite sand,
a fire borne over sea by wings of butterflies
smouldering in her hands.

3

You walk toward a door. She wakes.
She turns.

She does not turn to salt.

Out of causeless being,
again,
perceiver of the world.

She turns.
She lifts no veil.

Two stars
swing over the desert.

She turns.
You enter.

She speaks.

Corpus

So much in each stone.

The history of the world and more—
the blood of it, the vision of it.

See, here, the dreams of stone:
bone, flesh, wing, seed.

This stone heart
with all the hope
of life in it.

La Faccia

"Whose image sanctifies the game?"
—Charles Dickens, *The Old Curiosity Shop*

Kindly H., your beauty dyed to the bill remains.
What was dragged 'cross roads was superficial flesh.
Your son said 'flesh of flesh'.

Great men swam seas to you, made literature
for your face and the apparition of the face—
what the gods dub *il gioco.*

In all the colours of the night
the fairground lights your sprayed-on skin.
Modernity and the miracles.

Your doctor wrote: 'In lieu of dirt, what would we plough?
Without the bed, where would we kick?
Devoid of heart, why would we kill?'

Snow fell to bury his scattered limbs.
Hunched shoulders huddled in aspect mourning
the scene for *chi*?

So bad with names your mirror's inscribed.
This is no excuse
for abusing a child.

Accidents run in this family.
Return to the fringe of the world
where passers-by trade.

You Learn How Beautiful You Are

This morning you open your eyes.

It is like for the first time
you can feel the rain on your skin
when you look at it wetting the clear panes of the window.

Out of shadow comes light, more light,
and the walls fall away
and deer come to you and birds,
moths and the mouths of flowers,
attracted to light
not out of the sun or some high candle
but out of you, shining from you
and it may always have been there
but you'd never seen it.

It blinds you.

You stumble and catch rough bark,
inhale mulch and soil,
touch the wet roots of ferns,
their feathery leaves.

You hear something,
a sound like someone calling.

As If You Were Homeland

I will undress you as if you were ocean,
each wave a tongue on lit skin.

I will lick each salty wavelet
until you are naked as pearly shell,

polished and gleaming
cloud in its falling, reforming.

I will siren you as a mouth does
cornucopia, corn flesh,

feathers of turkeys and pheasants
braided in black hair.

There will be plenty that's fertile,
nourished by gut-blood and cow dung.

Bison will carry my heart
over mountain and prairie

hunting the wild, white crane.
I will fall down a hundred rivers,

heave up peaks bent on heaven
when nothing but climbing will do.

I will trespass your unexplored country,
cry out in your oldest forest.

I will love you as if you were homeland,
boundless and trembling in winds.

A Little Light

1

He starts with trees in the mist.
It might as well be a photograph
until you get close.

The gauzy slip of the girl's skirt just barely
visible
in whiteness.

The fact of words on the page,
the beginning and end.

He starts with trees in the mist,
bare branches.

See how the mist has wet
the skin of the branches,
how the bark of the birch
shines in the white dawn.

What has happened to the girl,
her face unrecognisably
washed in mist?

Milk splashed over newsprint.

The story fades away
in clumsy whiteness.

2

He starts with the pact we have made
that art is realistic.

He paints the girl first, then the trees.

He paints her red lips like the masters.

He paints the nipples on her breasts,
white handfuls of flesh.

He paints her muslin dress.

He paints the man in the distance.

He paints the man's tears.

He covers the scene in mist.

He paints the scene again.

He paints the scene many times,
each time losing the story
in some memory
through which we cannot see.

3

Through the mist,
just barely,
a candle glows beneath birch boughs.

Isn't the Start

Isn't the end, with its serried edge,
broke bottle neck, a glaze of blood,
so gently in, so smoothly out,
my friend, my friend,
isn't the end.

Isn't the core, with its poison seed,
brown secret rot, a veil of juice,
so hidden within, so bitten out,
my friend, my friend,
isn't the core.

Isn't the heart, with its fiery berth,
quaternate scheme, a flash of current,
so clamorous in, so silent out,
my friend, my friend,
isn't the heart.

Isn't the start, with its coming to,
unfolding wings, a bridge of seeing,
so dark within, so blazing out,
my friend, my friend,
isn't the start.

Person

I do not exist. I am nothing. I am not here.
I hold air, smoke, the sound of the sea. I wait.
I am where the bird was, what held the flower.
A sound came from me. And stars. And sunlight, rain.
I undo myself. I am as free as I can be, which is completely.

You do not exist. You are nothing. You are not here.
You hold air, smoke, the sound of the sea. You wait.
You are where the bird was, what held the flower.
A sound came from you. And stars. And sunlight, rain.
You undo yourself. You are as free as you can be, which is
    completely.

He does not exist. She is nothing. It is not here.
He holds air, smoke, the sound of the sea. She waits.
It is where the bird was, what held the flower.
A sound came from him. And stars. And sunlight, rain.
She undoes herself. It is as free as it can be, which is completely.

Sightings

1

Two kingfishers,
one mink.

Eleven ducklings, then four.
Wagtails, too many to count.
Blue tits, blackbirds.
A pair of swans.

A heron, in a tree.

2

A blackbird enters a hole in the old stone wall.
Clouds reflect in the river; forming, reforming.
A blackbird flies from the wall with an egg in its mouth.

Son

In my Father's house are many mansions: if it were not
so, I would have told you. I go to prepare a place for you.
— John 14:2, *King James Bible*

1

This is my body.

The pain in my hand is my tool, I work it.
It's a Fender Strat. I play it.
I look at myself. I'm expected. I expect
to hurt my hand,
to hurl the shovel, to dig.

I disappoint, I am disappointed. I shame,
I am ashamed. I walk, I am
asleep in bed as the earth
underneath
opens.

I am
working dirt from my eyes, fire
from my Cons. I am
holding my son to the light, looking
like a rabbi through temple skin
at the music in his head, wishing
I could take it out, hear
the songs he sings himself.

This is my bread.

2

World of flesh.
World of concrete.
World of voices.
World of text.
World of miracles.
World of vacuums.
World of turtlenecks.
World of hot boxes.
World of drawings.
World of proper names.
World of brooding.
World of drinking.
World of answers.
World of questions.

3

God isn't here to stake out dry tongues,
to lay claim to scorched fields of hay.

I stand in a field, rubber soles melting.
The wind is a cow.

There are words all around me, though everyone
is silent, threatening
to open my chest.

My family is looking,
mouthing the words they predict I will say.

"I can imagine how my lungs smell,
how my guts smell, how my heart smells,
but I don't want to know."

4

Who cries at night
Who cries in silence
Who cries uncomforted

When the dead is buried
his Parcheesi game
sits on the table
his half-smoked pack of Marlboro Reds
his half-drunk bottle of Labatt's

Who smokes the pack
Who kicks the bottle
to watch the foamy liquid pool

Who wipes the seat clean
of his last piss

Who kneels on the floor
reading the hieroglyphics
of his waste

5

An old Ford with flat tires
pulls past the window.

A Bayliner chops a girl's skin,
wheels on.

Water, rust-flavoured, leaks from the tap.

My bones are a Clydesdale,
my eyebrows an eagle.

Within my father's house,
I abide.

A man and woman doing love in a room
heady with the smell of red dirt spice.

Bent palms comb light.

Sweat between bellies and thighs
dissolves. How sweet
is life.

Revelation

The heron has a dream of blindness.

He starves, but it is beautiful;
the feeling of the fishes brushing his legs.

Lightning Source UK Ltd.
Milton Keynes UK
UKOW03f1154140314

228146UK00002B/26/P